The
BASIC
Book

W9-DBK-295

The
BASIC
Book

A Cross-Referenced Guide to the BASIC Language

Harry L. Helms

Technical Writer and Consultant

McGraw-Hill Book Company

New York St. Louis San Francisco Auckland
Bogotá Hamburg Johannesburg London Madrid
Mexico Montreal New Delhi Panama Paris
São Paulo Singapore Sydney Tokyo Toronto

Library of Congress Cataloging in Publication Data

Helms, Harry L.
  The BASIC book.

  Includes index.
  1. Basic (Computer program language) I. Title.
QA76.73.B3H447 1983   001.64'24   82-13976
ISBN 0-07-027959-4

  34567890   FGRFGR   89876543

ISBN 0-07-027959-4

The editors for this book were Stephen Guty and Charles P.
Ray; the designer was Elliot Epstein, and the production
supervisor was Paul Malchow. It was set in Melior by Achorn
Graphic Services.

Printed and bound by Fairfield Graphics.

Contents

Key Word
Ready Reference

Key words	Page number	Apple II Applesoft	Atari 400/800	Commodore PET	IBM Advanced Personal Computer	Radio Shack Level II	Radio Shack Extended Color	Texas Instruments 99/4
ABS	37	●	●	●	●	●	●	●
ADR	33		●					
AND	18	●		●	●	●	●	
APPEND	30							●
ASC	33	●	●	●	●	●	●	●
ATN	37	●	●	●	●	●	●	●
AUDIO	7						●	
AUTO	7		●		●	●		
BEEP	28				●			
BLOAD	7				●			
BREAK	7							●
BSAVE	7				●			
BYE	7		●					●
CALL	41	●			●			
CALL CHAR	43							●

Key Word Ready Reference (cont.)

Key words	Page number	Apple II Applesoft	Atari 400/800	Commodore PET	IBM Advanced Personal Computer	Radio Shack Level II	Radio Shack Extended Color	Texas Instruments 99/4
CALL CLEAR	7							●
CALL COLOR	43							●
CALL HCHAR	43							●
CALL JOYSTK	30							●
CALL KEY	33							●
CALL SCREEN	43							●
CALL SOUND	28							●
CALL VCHAR	43							●
CALL-151	7	●						
CDBL	37				●	●		
CHR$	33	●	●	●	●	●	●	●
CINT	37				●	●		
CIRCLE	43				●		●	
CLEAR	7,8	●	●		●	●	●	
CLOAD	8		●			●	●	
CLOADM	8						●	
CLOAD?	8					●		
CLOG	37	●	●					
CLOSE	29			●	●		●	●
CLR	8	●		●				
CLS	43	●			●	●	●	
COLOR	43,44	●	●		●		●	
CONT	8	●	●	●	●	●	●	
CONTINUE	8							●

Key Word Ready Reference (cont.)

Key words	Page number	Apple II Applesoft	Atari 400/800	Commodore PET	IBM Advanced Personal Computer	Radio Shack Level II	Radio Shack Extended Color	Texas Instruments 99/4
COS	37	●	●	●	●	●	●	●
CSAVE	8		●			●	●	
CSAVEM	8						●	
CSNG	37				●	●		
CVD	33				●			
CVI	33				●			
CVS	33				●			
DATA	28	●	●	●	●	●	●	●
DEF	37							●
DEFDBL	15				●	●		
DEF FN	38	●		●	●		●	
DEFINT	16				●	●		
DEFSNG	16				●	●		
DEFSTR	16				●	●		
DEFUSR	42				●		●	
DEL	8	●					●	
DELETE	8				●	●		●
DIM	15	●	●	●	●	●	●	●
DISPLAY	27							●
DLOADM	8						●	
DRAW	44				●		●	
DRAWTO	44		●					
DSP	29	●						
EDIT	9				●	●	●	

Key Word Ready Reference (cont.)

Key words	Page number	Apple II Applesoft	Atari 400/800	Commodore PET	IBM Advanced Personal Computer	Radio Shack Level II	Radio Shack Extended Color	Texas Instruments 99/4
ELSE	22				●	●	●	
END	21	●	●	●	●	●	●	●
EQV	18				●			
ERASE	16				●			
ERL	38				●	●		
ERR	38				●	●		
ERROR	22				●	●		
EXEC	42						●	
EXP	38	●	●	●	●	●	●	●
FILES	9				●			
FIX	38				●	●		
FOR . . . TO	22	●	●	●	●	●	●	●
FRE	34,38		●	●	●	●		
GET	34,44	●		●	●		●	
GOSUB	21	●	●	●	●	●	●	●
GOTO	21	●	●	●	●	●	●	●
GR	44	●						
GRAPHICS	44		●					
HCOLOR	44	●						
HEX$	38					●	●	
HIMEN	9	●						
HLIN . . . AT	44	●						
HOME	9	●						
HPLOT	44	●						

Key Word Ready Reference (cont.)

Key words	Page number	Apple II Applesoft	Atari 400/800	Commodore PET	IBM Advanced Personal Computer	Radio Shack Level II	Radio Shack Extended Color	Texas Instruments 99/4
IF . . . GOSUB	23	●		●		●	●	
IF . . . GOTO	23	●		●	●	●	●	
IF . . . THEN	23	●	●	●	●	●	●	●
IMP	18				●			
IN	30					●		
IN#	30	●						
INKEY$	34				●	●	●	
INPUT	28	●	●	●	●	●	●	●
INPUT#	28			●	●	●	●	●
INSTR	34				●		●	
INT	38	●	●	●	●	●	●	●
JOYSTK	30						●	
KILL	9				●			
LEFT$	34	●		●	●	●	●	
LEN	34	●	●	●	●	●	●	●
LET	14	●	●	●	●	●	●	●
LINE	44				●		●	
LINE INPUT	30				●		●	
LIST	9	●	●	●	●	●	●	●
LLIST	29				●	●	●	
LOAD	9	●		●	●			
LOG	38	●	●	●	●	●	●	●
LOMEN	9	●						
LPRINT	29		●		●	●		

Key Word Ready Reference (cont.)

Key words	Page number	Apple II Applesoft	Atari 400/800	Commodore PET	IBM Advanced Personal Computer	Radio Shack Level II	Radio Shack Extended Color	Texas Instruments 99/4
LPRINT USING	29				●			
MEM	38					●	●	
MERGE	9				●			
MID$	34	●		●	●	●	●	
MKD$	38				●			
MKI$	38				●			
MKS$	38				●			
MOTOR	9						●	
NAME ... AS	9				●			
NEW	9	●	●	●	●	●	●	●
NOT	18	●		●	●	●	●	
NOTRACE	9	●						
NULL	38		●					
NUM	9							●
OCT$	38				●			
OLD	10							●
ON COM(n) **GOSUB**	23				●			
ON ERROR GOTO	23				●	●		
ONERR ... GOTO	23	●						
ON ... GOSUB	24	●	●	●	●	●	●	●
ON ... GOTO	23	●	●	●	●	●	●	●

Key Word Ready Reference (cont.)

Key words	Page number	Apple II Applesoft	Atari 400/800	Commodore PET	IBM Advanced Personal Computer	Radio Shack Level II	Radio Shack Extended Color	Texas Instruments 99/4
ON KEY(n) GOSUB	24				●			
ON PEN GOSUB	24				●			
ON STRIG(n) GOSUB	24				●			
OPEN	29			●	●			●
OPEN COM ... AS	29				●			
OPTION BASE	16				●			●
OR	18	●		●	●	●	●	
OUT	29				●	●		
PADDLE	30		●					
PAINT	44				●		●	
PCLEAR	44						●	
PCLS	45						●	
PCOPY	45						●	
PDL	30	●						
PEEK	41	●	●	●	●	●	●	
PLAY	29				●		●	
PLOT	45	●	●					
PMODE	45						●	
POINT	45				●	●		
POKE	41	●	●	●	●	●	●	
POP	42	●	●					

Key Word Ready Reference (cont.)

Key words	Page number	Apple II Applesoft	Atari 400/800	Commodore PET	IBM Advanced Personal Computer	Radio Shack Level II	Radio Shack Extended Color	Texas Instruments 99/4
POS	34,38	●		●	●	●	●	●
POSITION	26		●					
PPOINT	39						●	
PR#	29	●						
PRESET	45				●		●	
PRINT	25	●	●	●	●	●	●	●
PRINT USING	26				●	●	●	
PRINT @	26					●	●	
PRINT #	27	●		●	●	●	●	●
PSET	45				●		●	
PTRIG	30		●					
PUT	45				●		●	
RANDOM	39			●		●		
RANDOMIZE	39				●			●
READ	28	●	●	●	●	●	●	●
RECALL	28	●						
REM	5	●	●	●	●	●	●	●
RENUM	10				●		●	
RESEQUENCE	10							●
RESET	10,45				●	●	●	
RESTORE	28	●	●	●	●	●	●	●
RETURN	21	●	●	●	●	●	●	●
RIGHT$	34	●		●	●	●	●	
RND	39	●	●	●	●	●		●

Key Word Ready Reference (cont.)

Key words	Page number	Apple II Applesoft	Atari 400/800	Commodore PET	IBM Advanced Personal Computer	Radio Shack Level II	Radio Shack Extended Color	Texas Instruments 99/4
RUN	10	●	●	●	●	●	●	●
SAVE	10	●		●	●			●
SCREEN	45				●		●	
SEG$	34							●
SET	45					●	●	
SETCOLOR	45		●					
SGN	39	●	●	●	●	●	●	●
SIN	39	●	●	●	●	●	●	●
SKIPF	10						●	
SOUND	29		●		●		●	
SPC	39			●	●			
SPEED	29	●						
SQR	39	●		●	●	●	●	●
STEP	22	●	●	●	●	●	●	●
STICK	30				●			
STOP	21	●	●	●	●	●	●	●
STORE	29	●						
STRIG	30		●		●			
STR$	35	●	●	●	●	●	●	●
STRING$	35				●	●	●	
SWAP	16				●			
SYS	10			●				
SYSTEM	10				●	●		
TAB	27	●		●	●	●	●	●

Key Word Ready Reference (cont.)

Key words	Page number	Apple II Applesoft	Atari 400/800	Commodore PET	IBM Advanced Personal Computer	Radio Shack Level II	Radio Shack Extended Color	Texas Instruments 99/4
TAN	39	●		●	●	●	●	●
TEXT	46	●						
TI	39			●				
TIMER	39						●	
TIME$	39				●			
TRACE	10	●						●
TROFF	10				●	●	●	
TRON	11				●	●	●	
UNBREAK	11							●
UNTRACE	11							●
UPDATE	29							●
USR	42	●		●	●	●	●	
VAL	35	●	●	●	●	●	●	●
VARPTR	35				●	●	●	
VERIFY	11			●				
VLIN . . . AT	46	●						
VTAB	46	●						
WAIT	21	●		●	●			
WHILE . . . WEND	24				●			
WIDTH	27				●			
WRITE	27				●			
XOR	18				●			

Preface

If Beginner's All-purpose Symbolic Instruction Code (BA-SIC) is not currently the most widely used computer language in the world, it is well on its way to becoming so. BASIC has many limitations compared to most other languages. However, it is easy to learn and use. Its simplicity made it a "natural" for use with the rapidly growing number of microcomputer systems.

Unfortunately, BASIC's popularity has come at the expense of uniformity. Many microcomputer manufacturers incorporate unique features in their implementations of BASIC. Technological changes have made possible certain features (such as graphics statements) not envisioned when John Kemeny and Thomas Kurtz developed BASIC in 1964 at Dartmouth College. The result is that one can be a proficient programmer in one dialect of BASIC yet have problems using a system with a different implementation of BASIC. This book addresses that problem. It covers the following implementations of BASIC:

- Apple II Applesoft
- Atari 400/800
- Commodore PET

- International Business Machines (IBM) Advanced Personal Computer
- Radio Shack Level II
- Radio Shack Extended Color
- Texas Instruments 99/4

This selection was based upon how widely an implementation is currently used (as in the case of Radio Shack Level II or Apple II Applesoft) or its potential for wide use (IBM Advanced, Radio Shack Extended Color, etc.).

This book includes the most commonly used features of each implementation of BASIC. However, it does not cover certain features of each implementation (such as disk operating system commands) which are unique to one microcomputer system. This book also assumes a familiarity with at least one of the implementations of BASIC covered.

I hope you will find this book useful both as a quick reference for the implementation of BASIC you normally use as well as those situations where you must work with an unfamiliar implementation or convert a program written in one version of BASIC into another.

Harry L. Helms

Converting from One BASIC Implementation into Another

A glance through this book will reveal many differences between the implementations of BASIC used by Apple, Atari, Commodore PET, IBM, Radio Shack, and Texas Instruments. Despite this, it will often be possible to "translate" a program written in one implementation of BASIC into another. Programs dealing with mathematical computations or data storage and manipulation will usually be easiest to convert; programs involving graphics, assembly language subroutines, or external file handling will present considerable (and sometimes insurmountable) conversion problems. Here is a systematic approach to converting different implementations:

- Scan the program you wish to convert for assembly language statements such as **PEEK, POKE, CALL, POP, USR**, etc. *Such assembly language routines will be difficult, if not impossible, to convert.* You will need memory maps of both microcomputers and should be able to use such maps. You will also need to know the instruction sets for the microprocessors involved and understand assembly language programming. If a program uses assembly language routines extensively, you will likely find it easier to write an entirely new program rather than convert the existing one.

- Examine the program for the following statements and functions, which have different meanings in various implementations. Refer to this book for the exact meaning in each implementation:

COLOR

DRAW

ERROR

GET

IF ... THEN

PEEK

POINT

PRINT USING

PUT

SCREEN

- As you go through the program, write down all variable names and what they represent.

- Break the program you wish to convert into functional blocks, such as input, computation, output, etc. A flowchart or written description of each block may be useful when working with longer programs.

- Graphics statements seldom translate into other implementations precisely. However, the effects of many graphics statements can be approximated on other systems by using graphics statements particular to that system. However, if a program uses elaborate graphics (such as those available on Apple, Atari, or Radio Shack Extended Color), it may be virtually impossible to reproduce or approximate them on systems using Commodore PET or Radio Shack Level II BASIC.

• A line-for-line conversion is usually inefficient and clumsy. It is better to convert each functional block using the special features and capabilities of the BASIC implementation you are converting to.

Syntax and Programming Practices

The following rules of syntax and programming practices apply to all implementations of BASIC covered in this book:

- Each line in a BASIC program must have a line number. Program execution begins with the lowest line number.

- Standard programming practice calls for using line numbers from 0 to 9999, increasing in increments of 10. Using increments of 10 allows inserting additional statements later if needed.

- Standard programming practice calls for using line numbers 0 to 999 for the main body of the program and line numbers over 1000 for subroutines.

- Explanatory remarks may be placed in a program using **REM** statements. **REM** statements do not affect program operation in any manner, although they still occupy space in memory. **REM** statements should be added as needed for clarity if the program listing is to be reviewed by others. They are useful for documentation in program development as well.

- More than one statement may be placed on a program line if the statements are separated by colons (:). (This feature is not available in Texas Instruments 99/4 BASIC.)

- Programs do not have to conclude with an **END** statement, although this is common programming practice.

- The main body of a program should be separated from subroutines with an **END** statement to prevent all subroutines from being executed following the conclusion of the main program.

System Commands

AUDIO Connects or disconnects cassette output to a television speaker (Radio Shack Extended Color only).

AUTO Automatically numbers program lines as they are entered from the keyboard (Atari, IBM Advanced, and Radio Shack Level II only).

BLOAD Loads binary data or machine language programs into memory (IBM Advanced only).

BREAK Sets up a breakpoint to halt program execution at a specified line number (Texas Instruments 99/4 only).

BSAVE Saves binary data onto a diskette (IBM Advanced only).

BYE Goes to calculator mode of operation from BASIC (Atari and Texas Instruments 99/4 only).

CALL-151 Puts system into monitor mode for machine language program execution (Apple II only).

CALL CLEAR Clears the video monitor screen (Texas Instruments 99/4 only).

CLEAR Sets all numeric variables to 0 and all string variables to null (Apple II and Atari only).

Sets aside a specified number of bytes of memory for string storage; also sets numeric variables to 0 and string variables to null (Radio Shack Level II and Extended Color only).

Clears all program variables and optionally sets memory area (IBM Advanced only).

CLOAD Loads a BASIC program from a cassette tape (Atari, Radio Shack Level II and Extended Color only).

CLOADM Loads a machine language program from cassette tape (Radio Shack Extended Color only).

CLOAD? Compares a program in memory to one on cassette tape. If there are differences, **BAD** will be displayed on the video terminal (Radio Shack Level II only).

CLR Same function as **CLEAR** (Apple II and Commodore PET only).

CONT Continues execution of a program after it has been halted (not available on Texas Instruments 99/4).

CONTINUE Same function as **CONT** (Texas Instruments 99/4 only).

CSAVE Saves a program in memory onto a cassette tape (Atari, Radio Shack Level II and Extended Color only).

CSAVEM Writes out a machine language file (Radio Shack Extended Color only).

DEL Deletes indicated program lines from a program. The form is

  DEL program line(s)

(Available in Apple II and Radio Shack Extended Color only.)

DELETE Same function as **DEL** (IBM Advanced and Radio Shack Level II only).

Deletes programs or data files from filing system (Texas Instruments 99/4 only).

DLOADM Loads machine language programs at baud

rate specified; 0 for 300 bits per second (baud) or 1 for 1200 baud (Radio Shack Extended Color only).

EDIT Allows editing of line number specified (IBM Advanced, Radio Shack Level II and Extended Color only).

FILES Lists files in diskette directory that match file name specified (IBM Advanced only).

HIMEN Sets addresses of highest memory address available during program execution (Apple II only).

HOME Moves cursor to top left of video display (Apple II only).

KILL Erases a diskette file (IBM Advanced only).

LIST Displays a list of all program lines specified. If no lines are specified, the entire program is displayed. The form is

> **LIST** first line number – last line number

LOAD Same function as **CLOAD** (Apple II, Commodore PET, and IBM Advanced only).

LOMEN Sets lowest address available in a program (Apple II only).

MERGE Merges saved program with one in memory (IBM Advanced only).

MOTOR Turns cassette recorder on or off (Radio Shack Extended Color only).

NAME . . . AS Renames a diskette file. The form is

> **NAME** old diskette name **AS** new diskette name

(Available in IBM Advanced only.)

NEW Deletes entire program from memory and clears all variables.

NOTRACE Turns off **TRACE** mode feature (Apple II only).

NUM Similar to **AUTO**, but begins line numbering at 100 and advances in increments of 10 (Texas Instruments 99/4 only).

OLD Similar function to **CLOAD** (Texas Instruments 99/4 only).

RENUM Renumbers program lines in specified increments. The form is

> **RENUM** new, start, inc

where *new* is the first new line number, *start* is the line number in the original program where renumbering is to start, and *inc* is the increment by which the renumbering increases. If *inc* is omitted, line numbers increase by 10 (IBM Advanced and Radio Shack Extended Color only).

RESEQUENCE Renumbers program lines in a specified increment beginning at indicated line number. The form is

> **RESEQUENCE** beginning line, increment

(Available in Texas Instruments 99/4 only.)

RESET Reinitializes all diskette information (IBM Advanced only).

RUN Begins program execution. If a line number follows, program execution begins at that line.

SAVE Same function as **CSAVE** (Apple II, Commodore PET, IBM Advanced, and Texas Instruments 99/4 only).

SKIPF Skips to next program on a cassette tape or to end of specified program (Radio Shack Extended Color only).

SYS Same function as **CALL-151** (Commodore PET only).

SYSTEM Same function as **CALL-151** (IBM Advanced and Radio Shack Level II only).

TRACE Indicates which line number in a program is being executed (Apple II and Texas Instruments 99/4 only).

TROFF Same function as **NOTRACE** (IBM Advanced, Radio Shack Level II and Extended Color only).

TRON Same function as **TRACE** (IBM Advanced, Radio Shack Level II and Extended Color only).

UNBREAK Ends breakpoint established by **BREAK** (Texas Instruments 99/4 only).

UNTRACE Same function as **NOTRACE** (Texas Instruments 99/4 only).

VERIFY Same function as **CLOAD?** (Commodore PET only).

Variables and Arrays

GENERAL RULES FOR VARIABLES

- All variable names must begin with a letter of the alphabet (A to Z).

- Another letter or a digit (0 to 9) may follow the letter.

- Variable names may contain up to 255 letters or digits; however, only the first two letters or digits will be "significant" in distinguishing between variable names. *Exceptions:* Variable names are significant to the first 15 letters or digits in Texas Instruments 99/4 BASIC; variable names are significant to the first 40 letters or digits in IBM Advanced BASIC.

TYPES OF VARIABLES

Different types of variables may be declared by adding the appropriate character following each variable name.

Character	Type	Definition
$	String	Variable containing up to 255 characters
%	Integer	Variable storing a whole number from -32767 to 32767
! or **E**	Single precision	Variable storing value using 6 significant figures
#	Double precision	Variable storing value using 16 significant figures
D	Double precision with scientific notation	Used for constants or for output for very large or very small numbers

Variables without declaration characters are assumed to be single precision.

ASSIGNMENT OF VALUES

Values may be assigned to variable names using the **LET** statement:

  LET X = 10

However, values may be assigned to variables without **LET**:

  X = 10

Values may be assigned to variables as the results of operations:

  X = A/B

ARRAYS

Arrays are items of data arranged and stored using a single variable name. The individual parts of an array are known as *elements*. Elements may be numbers or strings. Each element is identified by the array name followed by an integer (known as a *subscript*). Array names follow the same rules as variable names.

The number of elements in an array is set by the **DIM** statement. The statement

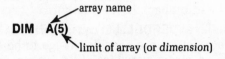

would set up a *one-dimensional* array containing the elements **A(0)**, **A(1)**, **A(2)**, **A(3)**, **A(4)**, and **A(5)**. The 0 subscripted variable name is usually not used but is available.

Arrays may have more than one dimension. The statement

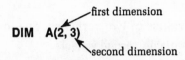

sets up a *two-dimensional* array with elements such as **A(0, 0)**, **A(1, 1)**, **A(1, 2)**, **A(2, 1)**, etc.

The dimensions of an array may be either numbers or expressions. **DIM** statements may be placed anywhere in a BASIC program.

SPECIAL VARIABLE STATEMENTS

DEFDBL   Causes variables beginning with any letter in a specified range to be stored and treated as double precision variables. The form is

   DEFDBL   letters

(Available in IBM Advanced and Rad:. Shack Level II only.)

DEFINT Similar to **DEFDBL**, but causes variables beginning with any letter in a specified range to be stored and treated as integer variables (IBM Advanced and Radio Shack Level II only).

DEFSNG Similar to **DEFDBL**, but causes variables beginning with any letter in a specified range to be stored and treated as single precision variables (IBM Advanced and Radio Shack Level II only).

DEFSTR Similar to **DEFDBL**, but causes variables beginning with any letter in a specified range to be stored and treated as string variables (IBM Advanced and Radio Shack Level II only).

ERASE Eliminates arrays of variables from a program (IBM Advanced only).

OPTION BASE Sets the lowest subscript limit of an array (IBM Advanced and Texas Instruments 99/4 only).

SWAP Exchanges values of two variables. The form is

    SWAP first variable, second variable

(Available in IBM Advanced only.)

Arithmetic, Relational, and Logical Operators

ARITHMETIC OPERATORS

+	Addition
−	Subtraction
*	Multiplication
/	Division
****	Integer division (IBM Advanced only)
∧ or ↑	Exponentiation
MOD	Gives integer remainder of integer division (Apple and IBM Advanced only)

RELATIONAL OPERATORS

<	Less than
>	Greater than
=	Equal to
<>	Not equal to

< =   Less than or equal to

> =   Greater than or equal to

(Not all relational operators are available in Atari or Texas Instruments 99/4.)

LOGICAL OPERATORS

AND   Expression is true if both parts are true; otherwise expression is false

OR   Expression is true if either part is true; otherwise expression is false

NOT   Makes an expression not true

XOR   Expression is false if both parts are false or if both parts are true; expression is true if one part is true and other part is false (IBM Advanced only)

IMP   Expression is false if first part is true and second part is false; otherwise expression is true (IBM Advanced only)

EQV   Expression is true if both parts are true or both parts are false; otherwise expression is false (IBM Advanced only)

NEGATION

An expression may be made negative by placing the symbol − before it.

ORDER OF OPERATIONS

Arithmetic, relational, and logical operations are performed in the following order of precedence:

1. Exponentiation
2. Negation
3. Multiplication and division from left to right
4. Addition and subtraction from left to right
5. Relational operators from left to right
6. **NOT**
7. **AND**
8. **OR**
9. **XOR**
10. **IMP**
11. **EQV**

The order of operations may be altered by placing expressions and operations in parentheses. When parentheses are nested, operations in the innermost set of parentheses are performed first. Evaluation is performed on the next level of parentheses outward, etc.

Control and Transfer Statements

UNCONDITIONAL CONTROL STATEMENTS

END Terminates execution of a program.

RETURN Ends a subroutine and returns control to the statement immediately following the last executed **GOSUB** statement.

STOP Interrupts execution of a program.

WAIT Suspends program execution until conditions specified following **WAIT** are met (Apple II, Commodore PET, and IBM Advanced only).

UNCONDITIONAL TRANSFER STATEMENTS

GOSUB Transfers program control to subroutine begin ning at line number indicated by expression following **GOSUB**.

GOTO Transfers program control to line number indicated by expression following **GOTO**.

CONDITIONAL TRANSFER STATEMENTS

ELSE Used in conjunction with the **IF** statement to specify an alternative action when the **IF** test is false:

       IF test   alternative action

IF A = B PRINT "A = B" ELSE PRINT "A DOES NOT EQUAL B"

(Available only in IBM Advanced, Radio Shack Level II and Extended Color only.)

ERROR Used in conjunction with **IF . . . THEN** to cause printing of an error message when a specified condition is found (Radio Shack Level II only).

    Simulates the occurrence of an error or allows definition of error codes (IBM Advanced only).

FOR . . . TO Sets up a loop of statements to be repeated for a specified number of times. The **FOR . . . TO** loop is terminated by **NEXT**:

```
10   FOR I = 1 TO 10
20   PRINT I;
30   NEXT
```

I is known as the *index variable*. Each time the loop is executed, 1 is added to the value of the index variable. When the value of the index variable exceeds the upper limit of its range (10 in the example above), execution of the loop ends and program execution continues normally.

    STEP may be used to specify the increment by which *I* increases. In the program line

```
10   FOR I = 1 TO 50   STEP 5
```

I will increase from 1 to 50 in jumps of 5 and the loop will terminate when the value of *I* exceeds 50. If **STEP** is omitted, *I* will increase in increments of 1. The increment, starting value, and ending value of *I* may be negative numbers.

IF . . . GOSUB Tests the expression following **IF** to see if it is true or false. If the expression is true, the subroutine beginning at the line number following **GOSUB** is executed. If the expression is false, the next line in the program is executed. (Not available in Atari, IBM Advanced, or Texas Instruments 99/4.)

IF . . . GOTO Tests the expression following **IF** to see if it is true or false. If the expression is true, program control is transferred to the line number following **GOTO**. If the expression is false, the next line in the program is executed. (Not available in Atari or Texas Instruments 99/4.)

IF . . . THEN Tests the expression following **IF** to see if it is true or false. If the expression is true, the statement following **THEN** is executed. If the expression is false, the next line in the program is then executed. An alternative action to the one following **THEN** may be specified by using **ELSE**:

> **IF A = B THEN PRINT "A = B" ELSE STOP**

(Texas Instruments 99/4 allows only line numbers following **THEN** and **ELSE**.)

ON COM(n) GOSUB Branches to subroutine beginning at line number following **GOSUB** when information enters the communications buffer through the communications adapter (1 or 2) indicated by n (available in IBM Advanced only).

ON ERROR . . . GOTO Transfers program control to line number following **GOTO** when error is found during program execution. The **ON ERROR . . . GOTO** statement must be executed before an error occurs to have effect (available in IBM Advanced and Radio Shack Level II only).

ONERR . . . GOTO Same function as **ON ERROR . . . GOTO** (Apple II only).

ON . . . GOTO Transfers program control to a line number depending upon an integer obtained by evaluating the expression following **ON**:

100   ON I GOTO 300, 400, 500
  when I   1   2   3

I is an expression evaluating to an integer. If the value of *I* is greater than the number of elements following **GOTO**, the next line in the program is executed.

ON ... GOSUB   Similar to **ON ... GOTO**, but transfers control to subroutines instead of line numbers.

ON KEY(n) **GOSUB**   Enables trap routine for a key specified by n, where n is an expression between 1 and 14 (IBM Advanced only).

ON PEN GOSUB   Transfers control to subroutine beginning at line number following **GOSUB** when light pen is activated (IBM Advanced only).

ON STRIG(n) **GOSUB**   Enables trap routine when one of the joysticks is pressed. If n = 0 the first joystick controls; if n = 2 the second joystick controls (IBM Advanced only).

WHILE ... WEND   Sets up a loop of statements which is executed as long as a given condition is true. The usual form is

    WHILE   expression
    Loop of statements
    WEND

The expression is true as long as it is not equal to zero. After each loop execution, the expression following **WHILE** is checked. If the expression is not true, program execution resumes at the first statement following **WEND** (IBM Advanced only).

Input and Output Statements

OUTPUT STATEMENTS

PRINT Outputs string variables, numbers, variables, or material enclosed in quotes:

```
100  X = 10
200  PRINT X
     10
100  A$ = "OUTPUT"
200  PRINT A$
     OUTPUT
100  PRINT "OUTPUT"
     OUTPUT
```

More than one item can follow a **PRINT** statement. If the items are separated by commas, each item is printed in a separate printing zone on the microcomputer system's video display:

```
100  PRINT "OUTPUT", "OUTPUT"
     OUTPUT          OUTPUT
```

If the items are separated by semicolons, no space is inserted between items on the display:

```
100  PRINT "OUTPUT"; "OUTPUT"
     OUTPUTOUTPUT
```

PRINT can also be used to perform calculations:

```
100   PRINT 5 = 2
           7
```

PRINT @   Specifies the exact position where printing is to begin. The usual form is

PRINT @   n, output

where n is an integer from 0 to 1023 and output is the data to be printed (Radio Shack Level II and Extended Color only).

POSITION   Similar function to **PRINT** @ (Atari only).

PRINT USING   Prints string and numeric values according to format specified. The form is

PRINT USING   format specifier; value

PRINT USING uses the following symbols in format specifiers:

#	Specifies position of a digit
.	Specifies the decimal point in a value
,	Specifies that a comma is to be inserted after every third digit
**	Specifies that all unused spaces to the left of the decimal will be filled with asterisks
$$	Specifies a dollar sign will occupy the first position preceding the number
**$	Specifies a dollar sign in the first position preceding the number and all unused spaces to the left will be filled with asterisks

∧∧∧ or ↑↑↑↑   Specifies that the value is to be printed in exponential form

+   Specifies a + for positive numbers and a − for negative numbers when placed at the beginning of the format specifier

/n/   Specifies that n plus 2 additional characters from a string are to be printed (IBM Advanced only)

%n%   Specifies a string field of more than one character; the length of the field will be the number of spaces equal to n plus 2 (Radio Shack Level II and Extended Color only)

!   Specifies that the first string character of the current value will be returned

(**PRINT USING** statement is available in IBM Advanced, Radio Shack Level II and Extended Color only.)

TAB   Used with **PRINT** to specify printing begins in a specified column position. The form is

     PRINT TAB (exp)

where *exp* is an integer or expression that evaluates to an integer (not available in Atari).

PRINT #   Prints the values of specified data onto a file or cassette tape (not available in Atari).

DISPLAY   Similar in function to **PRINT** (Texas Instruments 99/4 only).

WRITE   Similar to **PRINT,** but commas are inserted between items as they are output (IBM Advanced only).

WIDTH   Sets output line width in number of characters (IBM Advanced only).

INPUT STATEMENTS

INPUT Halts program execution and waits for input from the keyboard. A prompting message may be added in quotes; it will appear on the display. The form is

> **INPUT** "prompt"; variables

INPUT# Inputs data from a cassette and assigns it to variables (not available in Apple II or Atari).

RECALL Similar function to **INPUT#** (Apple II only).

READ Reads values accompanying a **DATA** statement and assigns them to specified variables. The form is

> **READ** list of variables

DATA Shows data in a list in a program. It can be accessed by a **READ** statement. The form is

> **DATA** list of items

READ and **DATA** statements are used together in the following manner:

This is the first value read for SUM	**100 READ SUM**	This is the second value read for SUM
	200 DATA 10, 20	
This is the third value read for SUM	**300 DATA 30, 40**	This is the fourth (and last) value read for SUM

RESTORE Causes the next **READ** statement to begin inputting data beginning with the first data item in the first **DATA** input.

SPECIALIZED OUTPUT STATEMENTS

BEEP Produces a "beep" sound from the speaker (IBM Advanced only).

CALL SOUND Selects sound output from the system (Texas Instruments 99/4 only).

CLOSE Closes peripheral data file (Commodore PET, IBM Advanced, Radio Shack Extended Color, and Texas Instruments 99/4 only).

DSP Displays line number where value of variable is changed (Apple II only).

LLIST Lists program or specified line on a printing peripheral (IBM Advanced, Radio Shack Level II and Extended Color only).

LPRINT Similar to **PRINT**, but sends output to a printing peripheral (Atari, IBM Advanced, and Radio Shack Level II only).

LPRINT USING Similar to **PRINT USING**, but with a printing peripheral (IBM Advanced only).

OPEN Opens a peripheral to input or output a data file (Commodore PET, IBM Advanced, and Texas Instruments 99/4 only).

OPEN COM . . . AS Opens data file for communications (IBM Advanced only).

OUT Sends specified value to a designated port (IBM Advanced and Radio Shack Level II only).

PLAY Plays music of a specified note, octave, volume and length (IBM Advanced and Radio Shack Extended Color only).

PR# Similar to **OUT** (Apple II only).

SOUND Produces specified tone for selected duration (Atari, IBM Advanced, and Radio Shack Extended Color only).

SPEED Selects speed at which characters are sent to an output device (Apple II only).

STORE Sends contents of a numeric array to a cassette (Apple II only).

UPDATE Reads and writes an opened file stored on a cassette (Texas Instruments 99/4 only).

SPECIALIZED INPUT STATEMENTS

APPEND Allows additional data to be added to the end of a data file (Texas Instruments 99/4 only).

CALL JOYSTK Checks for and accepts input from a joystick (Texas Instruments 99/4 only).

IN Goes to input port and receives value there (Radio Shack Level II only).

IN# Similar function to **IN** (Apple II only).

JOYSTK Returns the horizontal or vertical coordinate of a joystick (Radio Shack Extended Color only).

LINE INPUT Inputs line from keyboard to a string variable (IBM Advanced and Radio Shack Extended Color only).

PADDLE Accepts value from a control paddle (Atari only).

PDL Similar function to **PADDLE** (Apple II only).

PTRIG Returns a 0 if the game paddle button is presented or a 1 if it is not pressed (Atari only).

STICK Similar function to **JOYSTK** (IBM Advanced only).

STRIG Similar function to **PTRIG**, but is used with joysticks (Atari and IBM Advanced only).

Subroutines

A *subroutine* is a grouped sequence of statements accomplishing a certain action. A subroutine may be used as often as needed in a program.

THE GOSUB STATEMENT

Program control shifts to a subroutine through a **GOSUB** statement or a variant of **GOSUB**. When the subroutine is executed, program control shifts back (through a **RETURN** statement) to the main program at the first statement following **GOSUB**:

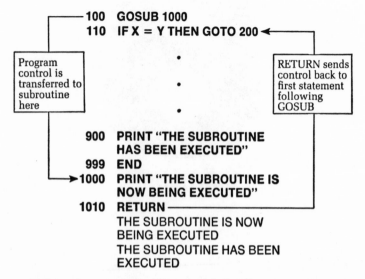

Subroutines are placed at the end of the main program. Good programming practice calls for using 0 through 999 for line numbers in the main program and 1000 through 9999 for line numbers in subroutines.

END should be added as the last statement in the main program when subroutines are used. This prevents program control from flowing directly to subroutines when execution of the main program is finished.

String Functions

The general form of a string function is

string function   (string variable or argument)

ADR Returns the address where the name, value, and pointer of the variable are located in memory (Atari only).

ASC Returns the American Standard Code for Information Interchange (ASCII) value of the first character of a string.

CALL KEY Checks keyboard and returns key being pressed or null string if no key is pressed (Texas Instruments 99/4 only).

CHR$ Returns a one-character string whose character has an ASCII graphics or control code specified by a number or expression evaluating to 0 through 255.

CVD Converts an 8-byte string to a double precision number (IBM Advanced only).

CVI Converts a 2-byte string to an integer (IBM Advanced only).

CVS Converts a 4-byte string to a single precision number (IBM Advanced only).

FRE Returns amount of free memory available for string variable storage (Atari, Commodore PET, IBM Advanced, and Radio Shack Level II only).

GET Same function as **CALL KEY** (Apple II and Commodore PET only).
   Reads a record from a random file into a random buffer (IBM Advanced only).

INKEY$ Same function as **CALL KEY** (IBM Advanced, Radio Shack Level II and Extended Color only).

INSTR Searches a designated string beginning at an indicated position for another designated string and returns position at which target string is found (IBM Advanced and Radio Shack Extended Color only).

LEFT$ Returns specified number of characters, n, from a string starting at the left. The form is
   LEFT$ (string, n)
(Not available in Atari or Texas Instruments 99/4.)

LEN Returns the length of a specified string or 0 if the string is null.

MID$ Returns specified number of characters, n, from a string starting at position p. The form is
   MID$ (string position, n, p)
(Not available in Atari or Texas Instruments 99/4.)

POS Returns a substring from a string beginning at position n in the string. The form is
   POS (string, substring, n)
(Available in IBM Advanced, Radio Shack Level II and Extended Color, and Texas Instruments 99/4.)

RIGHT$** Similar to **LEFT$, but returns specified number of characters from a string starting at the right (not available in Atari or Texas Instruments 99/4).

SEG$ Returns a specified number of characters, n, from a string beginning at position p, where p is a number representing a character numbered from left to right in the string. The form is

SEG$ (string, p, n)

(Available in Texas Instruments 99/4 only.)

STR$ Converts a numeric expression into a string.

STRING$ Returns a string of length n composed of a character c. The form is

STRING$ (n, c)

(Available in IBM Advanced, Radio Shack Level II and Extended Color only.)

VAL Converts a string to a number.

VARPTR Same function as **ADR** (IBM Advanced, Radio Shack Level II and Extended Color only).

Numeric Functions and Statements

The general form of a numeric function is

numeric function   (number or expression)

ABS   Returns the absolute value of an expression.

ATN   Returns the arc tangent of an expression.

CDBL   Returns a double-precision representation of the number or expression (IBM Advanced and Radio Shack Level II only).

CINT   Returns the largest integer not greater than the number or expression (IBM Advanced and Radio Shack Level II only).

CLOG   Returns the common logarithm of an expression (Apple II and Atari only).

COS   Returns the cosine of an expression.

CSNG   Returns a single-precision representation of a number or expression (IBM Advanced and Radio Shack Level II only).

DEF   Allows defining of new numeric functions (Texas Instruments 99/4 only).

DEF FN Same function as **DEF** (Apple II, Commodore PET, IBM Advanced, and Radio Shack Extended Color only).

ERL Returns the line number where an error has occurred (IBM Advanced and Radio Shack Level II only).

ERR Returns a value related to the code of an error (IBM Advanced and Radio Shack Level II only).

EXP Returns the value of the natural number *e* raised to the power specified by a following expression.

FIX Returns a truncated representation of an argument (IBM Advanced and Radio Shack Level II only).

FRE Gives the total number of unused bytes in memory. If followed by a string variable, gives amount of unused string space (Atari, Commodore PET, IBM Advanced, and Radio Shack Level II only).

HEX$ Returns the hexadecimal value of a number (IBM Advanced and Radio Shack Extended Color only).

INT Returns the integer portion of an expression that is less than or equal to the expression.

LOG Returns the natural logarithm of an argument.

MEM Returns the amount of free memory available (Radio Shack Level II and Extended Color only).

MKD$ Converts a double-precision number to an 8-byte string (IBM Advanced only).

MKI$ Converts an integer to a 2-byte string (IBM Advanced only).

MKS$ Converts a single-precision number to a 4-byte string (IBM Advanced only).

NULL Prints the number of spaces specified (Atari only).

OCT$ Returns the octal value of a number (IBM Advanced only).

POS Returns a number from 0 to 63 indicating the cursor position on the video terminal (Apple II, Commodore PET, IBM Advanced, Radio Shack Level II and Extended Color only).

PPOINT Returns color code of a specified graphics cell (Radio Shack Extended Color only).

RANDOM Reseeds the random number generator (Commodore PET and Radio Shack Level II only).

RANDOMIZE Same function as **RANDOM** (IBM Advanced and Texas Instruments 99/4 only).

RND Generates a pseudorandom number (not available in Radio Shack Extended Color).

SGN Returns a −1 if an expression is negative, a 0 if it is 0, and a 1 if it is positive.

SIN Returns the sine value of an expression in radians.

SPC Returns the number of skips specified (Commodore PET and IBM Advanced only).

SQR Returns the square root of an expression (not available on Atari).

TAN Returns the tangent of an expression (not available on Atari).

TI Sets real-time clock to specified value (Commodore PET only).

TIMER Returns contents of or allows setting of timer (Radio Shack Extended Color only).

TIME$ Sets or displays current time (IBM Advanced only).

Assembly Language Routines and Statements

DIRECT MEMORY ACCESS STATEMENTS

PEEK Returns the value stored at the address specified (Atari restricts use to video locations only; not available in Texas Instruments 99/4).

GO GCHAR Same function as **PEEK** (Texas Instruments 99/4 only).

POKE Places a specified value at a designated memory location. The form is

   POKE addr, val

where *addr* is the memory address and *val* is the value (not available in Texas Instruments 99/4).

ASSEMBLY LANGUAGE SUBROUTINES

CALL Causes program control to shift from the main program to the assembly language subroutine located at the specified memory address. The form is

   CALL memory address

Instructions to return to the main program are contained within the assembly language subroutine (Apple II and IBM Advanced only).

DEFUSR Defines the starting address of a machine language subroutine (IBM Advanced and Radio Shack Extended Color only).

EXEC Transfers control to assembly language programs located at specified address (Radio Shack Extended Color only).

POP Removes the most recent addition from the memory register stack (Apple II and Atari only).

USR Similar function to **CALL** (not available in Atari or Texas Instruments 99/4).

Graphics Statements

CALL CHAR Defines a new character for the video display (Texas Instruments 99/4 only).

CALL CLEAR Erases video display but does not affect program in memory (Texas Instruments 99/4 only).

CALL COLOR Defines the background color used by individual characters (Texas Instruments 99/4 only).

CALL HCAR Draws a horizontal line at a specified line number (Texas Instruments 99/4 only).

CALL SCREEN Defines background color of the video display (Texas Instruments 99/4 only).

CALL VCHAR Draws a vertical line at a specified column (Texas Instruments 99/4 only).

CIRCLE Draws a circle on the video display (IBM Advanced and Radio Shack Extended Color only).

CLS Same function as **CALL CLEAR** (Apple II, IBM Advanced, Radio Shack Level II and Extended Color only).

COLOR Sets the color of the point for the next plot (Apple II only).
   Defines the background color used for individual characters (Atari only).

Sets foreground and background colors (Radio Shack Extended Color only).

Sets the foreground, background, and border colors (IBM Advanced only).

DRAW Draws a line beginning at a specified starting point for a specified length and of an indicated color (Radio Shack Extended Color only).

Draws an object as specified by characters in the string following **DRAW** (IBM Advanced only).

DRAWTO Draws a line from the last plotted point to new position specified (Atari only).

GET Reads graphics contents of a rectangle into memory (Radio Shack Extended Color only).

In text mode, reads record from random file into random buffer; in graphics mode, reads points from an area of the screen (IBM Advanced only).

GR Turns on low-resolution graphics (Apple II only).

GRAPHICS Similar function to **CALL HCAR** (Atari only).

HCOLOR Selects the background color of the video display screen (Apple II only).

HLIN . . . AT Similar function to **CALL HCHAR** (Apple II only).

HPLOT Similar function to **DRAWTO** (Apple II only).

LINE Draws a line from one specified point to another (IBM Advanced and Radio Shack Extended Color only).

PAINT "Paints" video display starting at a specified point and continuing until a designated point is reached (IBM Advanced and Radio Shack Extended Color only).

PCLEAR Reserves specified amount of graphics memory (Radio Shack Extended Color only).

PCLS   Clears video display using specified background color (Radio Shack Extended Color only).

PCOPY   Copies graphics from source page to destination page (Radio Shack Extended Color only).

PLOT   Turns on specified graphics block (Apple II and Atari only).

PMODE   Selects graphics resolution and first memory page (Radio Shack Extended Color only).

POINT   Checks specified video location and returns a 1 if it is on, a 0 if off (Radio Shack Level II only).
Returns color of specified point on the screen (IBM Advanced only).

PRESET   Resets a point to specified background color (IBM Advanced and Radio Shack Extended Color only).

PSET   Sets a specified point to a designated color (IBM Advanced and Radio Shack Extended Color only).

PUT   Stores graphics from source onto start/end rectangle (Radio Shack Extended Color only).
In text mode, writes record from a random buffer to a random file. In graphics mode, writes colors onto specified area of screen (IBM Advanced only).

RESET   Resets a graphics point (Radio Shack Level II and Extended Color only).

SCREEN   Selects graphics or text screen and color (Radio Shack Extended Color only).
Returns the ASCII code for the character on the screen at a specified line and column (IBM Advanced only).

SET   Similar function to **PLOT** (Radio Shack Level II and Extended Color only).

SETCOLOR   Similar function to **CALL SCREEN** (Atari only).

TEXT Switches from graphics to text mode (Apple II only).

VLIN ... AT Similar function to **CALL VCHAR** (Apple II only).

VTAB Moves cursor down a specified number of lines (Apple II only).

Glossary

Address a label identifying the location in memory where information is stored.

ASCII acronym for American Standard Code for Information Interchange, a code used for data interchange between different computers.

Assembly Language a language using short phrases to produce machine language instructions.

Baud the rate of speed at which binary data is transferred, in bits per second.

Bit contraction of "binary digit," a unit of information equal to a single binary decision (0 or 1, true or false, etc.).

Bus circuit used as a path for data or power transmission.

Byte a unit of 8 bits.

Command an instruction directing a microcomputer to perform a specified action.

Compiler a system that converts a high-level language such as BASIC into assembly or machine language.

Execute to perform an instruction.

Floppy a flexible magnetic storage diskette.

Hardware the physical components of a computer system.

Instruction a statement containing information causing a microcomputer to perform a specified action, operation, or function.

Joystick a controller used to control video graphics.

Machine Language a language used directly by a microprocessor.

Memory part of a microcomputer where information is stored.

Microprocessor the microcomputer's central computational and control unit.

Modem an electronic device designed to connect computers and terminals over telephone circuits; a modulator-demodulator.

Paddle a graphics controller similar to a joystick.

Peripheral an adjunct device used with a microcomputer system, such as a printer, video terminal, etc.

Port an opening or connection for access to a microcomputer system.

Precision the exactness to which a quantity is defined or represented.

Program a set of instructions arranged in proper sequence for directing a microcomputer's operation.

Software programs, documents, procedures, and languages used with microcomputer systems.

Terminal a device in a microcomputer system where data can be stored or retrieved from the system.

Index

About the Author

HARRY HELMS is a technical writer and consultant. Formerly a technical writer for Radio Shack and Texas Instruments, he is the author of over 100 articles on various technical subjects for such magazines as *Popular Electronics*, *Science and Electronics*, *Elementary Electronics*, and *Modern Electronics*. He is the author of eight other books, and served as editor-in-chief of the forthcoming *McGraw-Hill Computer Handbook*. A graduate of the University of North Carolina, he lives in New York City.

Notes

Notes

Notes

Notes

Notes

Notes

Notes

Notes

Notes

Notes

Notes